Man on the Corner

Ryan Wilson

Table of Contents

Man on the Corner 2
Malta 5
2012 7

If...we Knew

If...we Knew 9
House of Glass 10
A Tree 11
Humanity 13
Sea Dawn 14
The World Keeps Turning 15
Weight of the World 16
Hope It Turns Around 17
Drift 18
Keep on Trying 19

Labyrinth

Labyrinth 21
Homecoming 22
Left Outside 24
Feels like Flying 26
Floating 27
Mirror 28
The Coast 29
Memory 30
Give A Little 31
Left My Heart 32
Lonely 33
Been Looking 34
Ten Miles 35
Tether 36
Moving Mountains 37
Crossroads 38
Hope is Gone 39
One More Step 40
Farewell 41

Peace

Peace 43
Walk in the Woods 44
Empty Streets 45
Thunderstorm 46
Concrete 47
Crashing Down 48
Back to Zero 49

Wild

Part I 51
Part II 55
Part III 57

Firework

Firework 61
Other Side 62
Man in the Mirror 63
Perfect 64
Automatic 65
The Fear 69
Tomorrow Can Wait 70
Sand 71
Chasing Rainbows 72
Free-Falling 73
The Flood 74
Simple Man 75
Go Get It 76
Watch the Sunrise 77

Introduction

Ryan is a young poet; he is only eighteen years old. He has spent his life living on a sailboat with his parents and younger brother, circling the globe one and a half times and in total sailing more than one hundred thousand miles across the open ocean. Travelling from country to country, in every corner of the world, and at the same time living in the confines of a small sailboat, sharpened the feeling and thoughts of humans' role and their responsibility for nature. All of this has influenced his poetry. Having limited attendance to public schools, he got his education through home schooling. Ryan has shown talents in math, drawing and painting, computer modelling in 3D and literature. His teachers/parents, both professors, organized a daily four-hour school.

His first poems were written when he was 12 years old. Since then he has written more than 150 poems, more than a half of these in the last two years.

The idea for this book was inspired by our friends, who after reading Ryan's poetry, felt that other people should read it too.

Father

Man on the Corner

There, on the corner, a man
Everyday, standing near the same garbage can
I always see him, every single day
Whenever I pass this way

Everyday-standing on the corner on the street
I wonder-Where does he sleep? What does he eat?
His clothes are clean but torn
And his shoes look quite worn
He just stands there
Not really looking any where

He seems to stare
Not noticing anyone
He just doesn't care
About what is said and done
He has that far away look in his eyes
I always thought it was some kind of disguise
But they never change
Not focusing on anything in range

Some people give him money
Some laugh as though he is funny
Some even try to talk
But most - around him they just walk

He doesn't see all these crowds
Just staring at the clouds
Some people say he is lazy
But again-most say he is just plain crazy

As for me, I don't really know
But winter has come and it has started to snow
Still he stands on the corner, alone
Not going anywhere, not going home

And there's a blizzard outside
While it's warm inside
Outside, it's twenty below
And there's already five feet of snow

That blizzard lasted all night
And come daylight
The snow ploughs come out
Pushing and throwing the snow about

I walk to that familiar street
On this day, there aren't too many people to meet
But I can't see that face
That used to be in this place
Of him, there isn't a trace

So I never found out what happened to that man
Who always stood near that garbage can
He just disappeared one cold and stormy night
Still don't know if everything turned out all right
Or if he just disappeared out of sight
But life went on
The years passing along
And whenever winter came with its icy toner
I remembered that lonely man on the corner.

Malta

Malta, Malta, what can I say?
Truly a one-of-a-kind place.
So many places to stay
And everywhere a friendly face.

An island of rock and sand
With little grass-covered land.
But blessed with deep sheltered ports:
Shelter from any storm.
Covered with massive forts
And as a bonus – it's always warm.

Many tried to take
Malta and nearly succeeded
But the final attack they couldn't make
And were always defeated,
Defeated by a few courageous men
Who were always outnumbered: one to ten.

Many a brave knight,
Shed his blood on Malta's stones.
Protecting his land, his family, his right;
And his aged bones
Still lay there – on Malta, his home
And he isn't lying there alone...

The mighty forts of Valletta and the surrounding countryside
Have stood for hundreds of years.
Many fearless souls have lived, fought and died
Facing god knows what kind of fears
As they defended their piece of wall
And never did they falter or fall.

So much history has seeped through
And Malta has caught every little bit.
Malta has changed – it's true
But none the worse for it.
Of course concrete has taken over
And everything is a bit closer.

Now Malta is a bustling city
With thousands of people and thousands of cars.
It's a charming place but not exactly pretty
And the sky – sometimes a smoke stain mars.
It's always filled with sound
And always movement all around.

It's true – skyscrapers grace the skyline
And buses roar down the street.
At night, halogen lamps shine
And the air isn't exactly sweet.
But Valletta continues to stand
And will stand until its walls are worn away,
Until its walls turn to sand,
And Malta will also stand until that day…

2012

I guess it's finally here,
Its day has finally come.
And are we really scared?
Scared of the end…and then some…?

People want to keep on believing,
That it'll get better, even though it's getting worse.
And who are we deceiving?
As we climb onto the global hearse…

We talk of global warming and going green,
Of electric cars and solar-powered ships.
All we DO is TALK – it's already obscene,
More so, when the earth finally rips.

We talk of making the world a better place
But it already sounds strange.
We keep on "saving" the human race,
All the while continuing our destructive rampage.

Sure, maybe everything will be alright…
And we've already seen the worst.
But it could happen and it just might…
Guess we'll have to see what happens on December 21st.

If...we Knew

If...we Knew

If we knew,
Would we stop? Would we stall?
Would we try something new?
Or would we say, "Forget it all"?

Would we try to change?
Change what we had become;
Would we act when hope is in range?
Or would we just pretend to act dumb?

Would we try to save?
Save our own skins,
From the cleansing wave,
That would erase us and our sins.

Would we run?
Would we hide?
Would we scream, "We're finished, done!"?
Would we give up inside?

Would we face our fate?
Or will we flee?
If we knew it was too late,
Could we realize? Could we see?

If we took a glance,
At all we had done.
If we had a second chance,
Another try, just another one.

Would we take?
What had been given to us.
Would we falter? Will we break?
And miss humanity's last bus.

If, we knew what to do?
Would we fulfil our task?
Would we take it all the way? Take it through?
Would we do it or just ask?
If we knew we had, just one more try,
Would we give it a shot? Or would we give up and die?

House of Glass

So fragile, so delicate,
That it trembles from every word spoken,
That it is the one and only fate,
That it is so easily broken,
That everything and everyone,
That everything said and everything done,
That everything reflects onto every wall,
And that someday it will have to fall.

You do not know it is there,
That it is listening to you,
That it is everywhere,
Always watching what you do.
Already it is starting to crack,
Nobody notices, they just let it pass,
But once it is done there is no going back
Because we live in a crumbling house of glass.

A Tree

Once there was a tree,
Who stood out, compared to other trees.
And when the wind blew from the sea,
Only his treetop could feel the breeze.

Years came and went,
Lightening, wind and rain,
Branches broken and bent,
But the tree observed his weaker counterparts with disdain.
Storms broke young saplings, ripped leaves
And even toppled some of the older trees.

But one fine morning,
Just another day, sunny and boring.
A hollow thumping sound was heard,
Cracks and a crash reverberated in the still air.
The trees passed around the word-
Woodcutters were finally here.

One by one they fell,
The young and the old,
Now nobody could tell
What the future would hold,
For trees continued to die,
Feeding the humans' fathomless supply.

Soon there was only one tree left,
Standing in an empty field,
But he knew he couldn't cheat death
No matter how much armor he could wield.
So on that misty day-so grey,
They came to take him away.

They came - carrying that fearful tool,
They marked him, right near the base.
This old tree was no fool,
He knew, of him there wouldn't be a trace.
And so they started to chop,
Wood began to splinter and pop.

He shook, he swayed,
But there was no repelling the attack.
As much as he wished he could've stayed,
It still ended in a mighty crack.
All his thoughts still unspoken,
He fell down - his back broken.

Facing an end so grim,
Lying face-down on the ground;
They started to cut, they started to trim,
Filling the mists with sound.
And the last thing he saw
Was the sharp-toothed blade of a hand-saw.

Piece by piece - they carried him away,
Away from an empty field, where trees used to stand,;
Never again, will this tree see the light of day,
And all of it…was done by humans' hand.

Humanity

Good-bye, humanity, good-bye!
All I ever did for you was try
Try to make it a better day
A better day for you
But all you ever did was throw it away
No matter what I tried to do

I tried to make this planet a better place
Better for the human race
I gave you all you ever needed
But you turned a deaf ear
No matter how much I pleaded
You didn't even care

Still after all of this, I gave you another try
Another try-so you could hear my plea
But you just said, "Good-bye!"
And wouldn't listen to me
So I gave up the fight
Letting you decide what was wrong or right

After all the pain,
I was back to the start-again
After all I tried to do
Now I ask myself-what have I done?
I tried to save you
Tried to save you from what you had become
And finally the burning sun sets in the sky
Good-bye, Humanity, Good-bye!

Sea Dawn

Sails on the horizon,
A gentle breeze is blowing
And the sun is rising
Its edge already showing.

It truly is fascinating:
Watching from the beach.
It has no rating:
Beyond criticizing, beyond reach.

Seagulls in the pinkish-blue sky:
Scavenging for an edible scrap.
Screaming as they fly:
Never taking a nap.

Ships steaming by:
Smoke pouring from their funnels,
Polluting the pristine sky,
Loaded to the gunnels.

The swell gently rolling on,
On to the shore.
All the wind is all but gone
But swell – always more…

Sunlight reflecting:
Off a plastic bottle, a Coca-Cola can.
The sea we're neglecting,
Loitering while we get a free tan.

So many things you can see,
While sitting still
And watching the sea:
The sea we're trying to kill…

The World Keeps Turning

We live, we die,
We leave fires that burn;
We pollute the sky,
But the world's still here, turn after turn.

Treating the earth like an experiment,
Not caring what happens after.
To us- it's just irrelevant:
Whether it'll be crying or laughter.

Cutting the trees,
Digging the dirt,
We melt, we freeze,
Not caring who we hurt.

We created heaven,
We created hell,
Slaughtering out own brethren;
Who said things were going well?

We created suffering and pain;
Then created the cure.
Are we not all insane?
Purging everything pure.

Nothing left anymore:
What are we doing?
What are we here for?
And what are WE proving?

We travelled into space,
We walked on the moon,
Discovered every possible place;
There's going to be nothing left-soon.

Everything we plunder, we destroy,
Everything in our path is left wrecked and burning,
We don't feel anymore, no happiness, no joy.
And after what has been done, the world is still turning.

Weight of the World

The weight of the world rests on my shoulders
Pulling me down like a bag of boulders
Struggling against the weight
Hearing all those say, "It's too late!"

Lately, the world has become so hot
Don't know if I can stand it or not
And every time I stumble
The world starts to crumble

Suddenly the world opens up a crack
And burning fire spills on my back
Don't know if I can stand it anymore
Because it never did this before

But still I carry the world around
All the while getting pushed into the ground
And nobody knows I'm here-down below
But the day will come along
When everybody will know
That I was the one that held out so long

Even with all the world pressing down on me
I held on long enough, so everyone could see
That I was the one
And now... my 'job' is done.

It has to go the other way,
Can't keep sliding down this slope.
Maybe tomorrow, maybe the next day:
Hoping it will get better; hoping
against hope.

It will turn,
Shift into reverse.
All good will return,
By the time I finish this verse…

Hope It Turns Around

Good must prevail!
It will get better, it will!
Still trying to no avail
But there's just one more hill…

It has to go – all this sorrow:
Leave this place, leave this ground.
Maybe today, maybe tomorrow,
But it has to turn around…

Drift

Drift, drift and drift
On these ocean, as they shift
This little piece of wood
Just drifting for no particular reason
Not bad, nor good
Just drifting, season after season

The wind blows it this way and that way
And the waves toss it around-day after day
But this little piece of wood doesn't care
Nor wind, nor waves, won't give it a scare
It's all beaten up and rotten
Thrown away and forgotten

Just drifting out there
Just drifting without a care
It doesn't disappear, it doesn't sink
It doesn't sail, it doesn't think
It's just one of man's many gifts
Upon the sea, still it drifts.

Keep on Trying

We've got to do something
Can't lie down and do nothing
Get up, stand up and do
Something to pull through

We can't sit around and forget
That we're not gone…yet
And if we take a glance
We still have a chance
To save what's left,
That it doesn't have to end
In destruction and death.
We have to watch our flag ascend
Back towards the sky,
All we have to do is try…

Everything we did, everything we made,
We can't just let it fade.
We just can't keep on giving up and crying,
So get up and keep on trying.

Labyrinth

Labyrinth

Roaming endless tunnels
They get narrower near the end
And into these endless funnels
I always seem to descend

Can't walk upright anymore,
Everything pressing down on me
The ceiling gets closer to the floor
And all this I sense, because I cannot see

No light at all
Everything's pitch black
And I slam into a wall,
When I try to go back

Keep hitting my head on low beams
Every time it brings a jolt of pain
And all those lost hopes and dreams
Come rushing back to me again

Still can't figure out yet,
How I fell into this pit?
Tangled in this endless net,
How was I caught in it?

Trying to find a way out,
I claw at the walls; I tear at the ceiling,
I scream and shout, I jump about
But I have no strength, no feeling

Running in all directions
No escape out of this living hell
Keep seeing endless reflections,
Of my life…if it had turned out well

Trying to escape, to run
But I get dragged back in
No light, no air, no sun,
And everything, again, I have to begin

These tunnels don't end, they don't stop
I can keep running until I drop
But anyway, I don't have a light to follow,
So I dwell in this labyrinth of misery and sorrow.

Homecoming

Not a soul in sight
Rolling plains as far as the eye can see
Walking day and night
But that doesn't matter to me

Doesn't matter that I've walked for five days
Travelling-using all the possible ways
It doesn't matter that I'm alone
It doesn't matter because I'm going home

Home, home at last
Long have I dreamt about this in the past
Imagined it in my mind
To return-to what was left behind

The grass is green
Trees are few to be seen
But I don't notice anything except this dirt track,
Because I'm coming back

Back to the place
From which I came
Back home-to see a familiar face
Back home- where everything was always the same

Suddenly a familiar tree
And there's a familiar post
And then I finally see
What matters the most

I walk through the gate
I can't breathe anymore
Hoping, praying-that I haven't come too late
And with those thoughts, I open the door.

Left Outside

They closed the door
And left me outside.
Don't they want me anymore?
Not letting outside…

Everything was so great.
They said I was the best,
There was no debate.
Who knew it would turn into this mess?

They stroked me, gave me a treat.
Always had a warm, cozy bed
And plenty of food to eat,
Although I never understood what they said…

It was like living in paradise,
Everything was done for me.
Daily strolls had to suffice
But I felt so free.

Time passes this way,
Everything staying the same.
And I cherished every day…
But finally my moment came…

They just decided to leave,
No warning, nothing at all.
I was dumped to grieve
And left in appall…

Now I sit in the deadening cold,
Covered in ice and snow
With nowhere to go,
Had I grown so old...?

And I don't feel myself freezing,
Don't feel my limbs go numb,
Don't hear myself sneezing,
Don't realize that they'll never come...

But still I sit in front of the door,
Hoping they'll let me inside.
Although there's not much to hope for...
Since I was left outside.

Feels like Flying

On the very top, I stand
Above the snow, right on the edge
Even soaring eagles cannot understand,
How could I get to this ledge?
From here, I see a rivers' birth
And thunders landfalls of rock and earth.

Here clouds move silently below me,
Through them waterfalls are heard,
Rushing over cliffs I do not see,
Lower down-a clump of moss, a lone bird,
Then a cluster of shrubs, some greenery,
And deer leaping amongst the beautiful scenery.

And here people find a home,
Shepherding mountain sheep,
Here they live all alone
Watching their herd climb over every stone heap.
Below them-a mighty river tries to use its mass,
To break out of a subduing, rocky pass.

From the mountain I see all of this
And there's nothing my eyes miss
Hearing the howl of tremendous river,
And the freezing wind makes me shiver.
On par with the eagles in the sky.
Far from everything, I feel like I can fly.

Floating

Floating away,
Day after day,
Waves wash over,
The land never gets closer.

Cannot sink,
Cannot swim,
Can only think
Of the ocean's next whim.

Carried by the tide,
Carried by every wave,
Already nothing left inside,
Nothing left to save.

The tide surges back and forth,
First south, then north,
It gets closer-the shore,
Can almost reach
The inviting beach
Trying to swim some more.
But the tide turns
And all the water returns.

Floating away again,
Away from land,
Back to the pain…
Nothing left to understand.

Repeated - over and over, nobody could stay sane
Floating on an expanse of blue and grey.
The wind whips up the waves-it's raining again.
Just floating… floating away.

Mirror

Mirror, hanging upon a wall
Seems to tell everything worth to know
But really nothing at all
Just hanging on the wall for show

In the reflection you seem to see
Everything you are
And everything you can be
But don't go that far
Because the mirror might be deceiving you
And you'll never know what to do

In the mirror, don't trust
Do what you must
But the mirror won't be able to see
What's really inside you or me

Still the mirror hangs upon a wall
Telling everything but nothing at all
Trying to look inside
But what's in there, is for you to decide.

The Coast

Rocks, waves, sand...
Where water borders land...
Where sea gulls fly...
Where the sea meets the sky...

Here lie the bones of ships lost
Along with sailors who tried to save them at all cost
Always so fascinating, so enticing
Ships doomed, before even realizing

The waves grinding stones,
Different colors but the same dull tones
Mighty boulders one day
Tiny pebbles the next
Always moving - without any rest
Moving...this way, that way

Always in motion
Powered by an unending ocean
Waves never straying off course
Invisible but still a relentless force

The sight, the feeling, the sound,
Waves pounding - felt even through the ground
And everybody knows it, or at least most
That they are facing the coast.

Memory

Memories are all that left
Everything else disappeared into some mysterious cleft
No matter how smart I was, no matter how deft
Memories are all I have left

Everything else was swept away
Gone - in a single day
No matter how hard I tried
Of everything else I was deprived

The present is gone
The future isn't there anymore
What's going on?
What's this for?

But my memories are still here
Not that I really care
Since everything else was lost
And memories don't repay that cost

Still memories are all that's left
One thing that wasn't swept away
Swept away - back to another day
And now, memories are all I have left.

Give A Little

Give me a little –
Doesn't matter if it's small or brittle.
Just something to call my own,
My piece of the world: my throne.

Give me a little piece –
A little piece of land.
Where I can live in peace:
But who would understand?

Give me something simple and small –
Nothing fancy, nothing rich.
I'm not asking for it all…
So what's the hitch?

Give me somewhere I can settle –
I don't want to trouble anyone.
Just want to sit and boil tea in a kettle,
While I watch the setting sun.

So what's the problem, what's the debate?
All my life I've had to roam
And all the time I've had to wait:
Wait for something to call my home…

Left My Heart

I left my heart behind,
Left what had almost become a home.
Must have been out of my mind
And now I'm all alone...

I left my heart
And sailed away.
Didn't know I had to part,
Until today.

In one short year,
I actually felt like someone.
Never thought I would get here
But when I did...again I had to run .

All of a sudden, it had all ended
And started to reverse.
I had become somewhat dependant
And now I felt even worse…

I had started to feel,
Something had started to matter.
Didn't want to see what was real
'Cause I knew it was going to shatter…

And it ended the same,
The same way it always does.
I saw, I sailed, I came
Then faded without a buzz…

And as I watched it fade,
Fade away into the haze,
I thought of all the friends I had made
And gave it one last gaze…

Now it's all back,
Back to where it used to be.
Me on my lonely track
With only water around me…

Not even a proper farewell for you
Before our ways we had to part.
And who ever knew?
That I would leave a piece of my heart…

Lonely

Lonely, so lonely
Just me and me only
Just like sitting on a barren rock
In a barren sea
Time goes by, watching it tick-this clock
And still there are no ships to see

It's hard to hold on
The wind howls, the waves try to sweep me
away
And when almost all life is gone
The sun rises - a new day
Another day of burning sun, of drenching rain
Another day, to bring back the pain

Sitting here all alone
Stranded a long way from home
Just me and me only
Makes me so lonely.

Been Looking

I've been looking ahead,
I've been looking back,
Looking at things said,
At a winding, broken track.

I look for tomorrow
And hit a solid wall.
I look at yesterday-nothing but sorrow
Disappearing into a never-ending hall.

I've been looking at today
But there's nothing to see.
And what can I say?
When there's nothing around me.

And what can I do?
When there's nothing left around
How can I break through?
When there's no light, no sound.

And how can I try?
To keep looking for
Something, in a sky
That isn't there anymore.

Ten Miles

Ten miles to this place
Walking at this relentless pace
The distance seems nothing at all
But I'm still walking - ready to fall

All the signs I see in the snow
Keep telling me to go,
Go on, dodging snow piles
And every sign says it's still ten miles

All the signs I see in the snow
Keep telling me to go,
Go on, dodging snow piles
And every sign says it's still ten miles

Wind turning snow into every kind of shape
Closing in on me - there is no escape
No escaping these snowy claws
No escaping these imaginary jaws
Every victim succumbs to their wrath
Everyone who walks this barren path

You know this is all in your head
But how would you know where to tread?
And I will myself to walk faster
But the snow feels like a sandblaster
And the harder I try
The faster I seem to die…

So I walk through this snow
I can't see, I don't know where to go.
All those signs, decorated with frozen smiles
Still keep telling me: it's only ten miles.

Tether

It jumps through the air
Wants to break free
But it's still there:
Chained to a tree.

The more it tries to fight,
The tighter the chain around its neck.
It can't breathe, it loses its sight:
Until it becomes nothing more than a sniveling
wreck.

No teeth left
From trying to bite through steel
No more can its own body it heft
Just bones – skin starting to peel.

Everytime it tries to make a move
The chain bites in, drawing blood.
Nothing and nobody to soothe
Its limp body – covered in mud...

Still it tries to break free,
Trying every day, no matter the weather
And it still doesn't see
That it can't break the tether...

Moving Mountains

Trying to break through,
Trying to shift these heavy rocks.
But whatever you do,
You can break out of this box.

You dig, you blast,
With everything - you attack
But just as fast
It comes tumbling back.

You use your pick, you use your spade,
Trying to blaze a trail,
That cannot, that will not, be made
Trying - although you're doomed to fail.

You hammer, you pound,
Attempting to break down the door.
And as you strike the ground,
You wonder - what am I doing this for?

Crossroads

There comes a time,
When decisions have to be made.
When life shifts on a dime
And dreams start to fade…

There comes a day,
When you come to an intersection.
When you just can't stay:
You have to choose a direction.

There comes an hour,
When you don't have time to think
And you have to use everything within your power
Just to keep from toppling over the brink…

It's not an easy choice to make
But you have to reach a decision.
Which road should you take,
When there's no time for precision?

Which path should you choose?
All these thoughts running through your head.
So much you stand to lose,
As you try to remember what someone once said…

And still you stand in front of the signpost,
Trying to make up your mind.
You think of what matters most,
Make a choice and wonder what you will find…

Hope is Gone

Hope is gone,
It was turned off, when it was on
All that I hoped for
Isn't there anymore
Gone forever
Likely never
To return
Because life took a different turn
Hope is gone, with it the light
Everywhere black as night
Nothing to see, nothing to hear
Nothing out there
Shattered dreams
Lost in shadowy realms
Wandering lost lands
Amid a sea of sands
Desert as far as the eye can see
Oh! Hope rescue me
Oh! Hope don't abandon me!
Sitting here all alone
'Cause, hope is gone

One More Step

One more step, one more pace,
Just one more.
I can finally finish this race,
And have something to live for.

But I guess I must've run out of luck
'Cause my feet seem to be frozen, stuck.
As if I stepped into glue,
I can't move and there's nothing I can do.

Like a fish on a hook,
I flop all about,
But whatever I try, wherever I look,
I just can't get out.

Like a bear caught in a trap,
I claw and I snap.
But I cannot break free,
And nobody cares about my plea.

Like a tiger in a cage,
I try to bend every steel bar,
Roaring and ripping in my rage,
But I know I won't get very far.

And just when I thought I was number one,
Everybody starts passing me.
Just when I was almost done,
I can't break free.

Now everybody has raced past,
And again - I am the last.
Now my feet aren't glued anymore,
But there's no race now, nothing to race for.

I drop to my knees,
Wondering why my feet decided to seize.
Just when I was so close,
What kept me back? Who knows?!?

Just when I was so close to success,
When I just had to finish this race.
And although my feelings I won't express,
I'll always know that there was only one more pace.

Farewell

Farewell, deep blue sea
The last time before me
You spill your blue tears
And at this woeful sight, again my fear appears

Like a friends' last plea
A plea that brought back the pain
Your sad whisper, calling for me
Knowing I will never see you again

My soul is racked as you plead
Remembering how many times I walked this shore
Wandering in the fog - taking time to heed
Your every summon - but not anymore

How I loved your silent sound
In the evening hours
Silence all around
Then suddenly the wind blows and the wave towers

You waited, you called…I didn't know what to do
But my soul couldn't hold on
I had to see you
And I returned to all that was gone

The world was empty…for me
Would you carry me away, mighty ocean?
I didn't hear, I didn't see
But at least I had your everlasting motion

Farewell, deep blue sea!
I won't forget what you were to me
And long after I'm gone
I'll remember your voice - remember…on and on…

Peace

Peace

Birds singing in the trees
Seagulls wheeling in the sea breeze
Animals hunting in the forest
The world's at peace, at rest

Suddenly shots are fired
Then birds fall out of the sky
More shots and more animals die
All of a sudden - peace has expired

More explosions: all around
Everything keeps falling to the ground
The peaceful silence is shattered
Nothing left of what mattered

The earth seems to crack
All those trees burned
The skies are increasingly black
As if the world never turned

The green grass is gone
The oceans are boiling
The sun doesn't rise at dawn
And it just gets more foiling

No more forests where once birds sang
No more streams running over the rocks
The only noise that's heard is - bang, bang
Only things in sight are big shiny blocks

Suddenly an explosion, a white light
Everything disappears in a flash
Blinding fire lights up the night
Everything obliterated with a horrendous
crash

And then there's silence – not a sound
The sky is grey - it starts to rain
Thoroughly soaking the scorched ground
And finally, there's peace again.

Walk in the Woods

The sir is so fresh,
Trees reaching for the sky,
Entwined-like a green mesh,
Like a roof-way up high.

Trees standing - so silent,
Moving their leaves, with a slight hiss,
Always there, always reliant.
And their eyes never miss,
What happens around,
Everything that walks the ground.

It's like another world, another space,
So peaceful, so quiet,
Better than any other place,
No people, no cars, no riot.
Just trees, trees, and trees,
With their branches and leaves.

But at the same time - so alive,
Full of wildlife, filled with natural things,
Calling to each other, trying to survive.
A wolf howls, a bird sings,
They are just living
In a haven the forest is giving.

But as I walk on,
There seems less life,
All the green seems to be gone,
Trees scarred, as if by a huge knife.
The forest becomes dull and grey,
Neither bird, nor beast comes this way.

There's a heavy noise in the air,
An assaulting, resonating sound,
Behind those dying trees over there,
The air hums, it vibrates the ground.
As I walk, trash crumples underfoot,
The air is hard to breath, heavy with soot.

I face the chemical-filled breeze,
My eyes blinded by acres of shiny glass,
Standing on what used to be acres of grass,
A city: standing on the skeletons of trees.

Empty Streets

Wandering empty streets
In a totally empty town
Empty cars with empty seats
Empty, broken houses - everything rundown

Rubble clutters the street
Nowhere to put ones feet
Nothing left alive
Nothing left…that could survive

Amid this cratered wasteland,
Where mighty building used to stand
Lie mighty piles of rubble
Wreckage and mayhem - nothing but trouble

Where people used to live, to eat, to sleep
And now all of this is left in a heap
People's lives snuffed out in an instant
Now everything seems so distant

All of it's empty, devoid of inhabitation
It's deserted - no population
And destruction and death
Are the only things left…

Everything empty, everything destroyed
Everything twisted, even solid metal sheets
Nothing left- to be enjoyed
Just an empty town with empty streets.

Thunderstorm

On this clear and sunny day
A thunderstorm is on the way.
Extinguishing the suns' last ray
And chasing everything and everybody
away.

It lumbers through,
Not caring what or who,
Gets caught under
This storm of lightning and thunder.

And as it approaches:
Everything goes dark, a draft of hot air.
Everything is silent – as it encroaches.
You can feel it in your hair.

Lightning flashes,
Illuminating the dark cloud,
Thunder crashes
Ever so loud.

Then comes the rain,
Roaring like an express train,
With the wind by its side
As it drives anybody left, inside.

Underneath the rain, lightning and thunder,
The wind trying to rip everything asunder,
Assaulted from every direction
With nothing to offer protection.

Lightning strikes all around,
The thunder seems to shake the ground.
The rain continues to pour
And the wind continues its tug-of-war.

Suddenly it's over, it's done,
Wet leaves catch the first glimpse of the sun,
Birds start to sing,
As if there wasn't anything.
The thunder seems like a muffled blast –
It's over and only fifteen minutes have gone
past.

Concrete

Nothing else to see
Except box upon box.
What else is there for me?
Except crushed rocks…

Why did I come to this place?
To "our future"…or so they say.
Not one remotely recognizable face,
Who would want to stay?

Every corner I turn,
Every street I cross,
Gives me nothing in return
And I become more and more at loss.

Lost in a concrete maze,
Every intersection exactly the same,
And I can't see through the haze,
Can't tell from where I came…

Metal, concrete and glass
Have become the earth, the land…
But who needs soil? Who needs grass?
Who needs all that, when we have homes built of sand?

All you need is that grey powder
And your life is complete.
You're talking…? Talk louder!
Because out there, whoever you're going to meet
Will surely be made out of concrete…

Crashing Down

We don't know what we're doing
We're just digging ourselves a hole
To fall into, and that's our only goal
Even though we think everything is improving

Burying ourselves with our own creations
The sky gets smaller and smaller
As the piles of garbage get taller and taller
And buried underneath - whole nations

And we just keep on creating,
More and more stuff
Not knowing it's already enough,
Enough of everything but it's no use debating

We just don't know when to stop
When to quit the wasting
And it seems that we are hasting
Towards the inevitable drop

We don't know it yet but we're tumbling out of the sky
Into the darkness below - we can already say good-bye
Because every person, every country, every town
Is already crashing down...

Back to Zero

Back down this road
Back to this time
And nothing ever showed
Neither a nickel, nor a dime

Back to the life I never knew
Back to the beginning, to the start
Back to the place I've never been too.
I might be going back but not my heart.

Back to zero, back to the starting line,
Back to what was once home,
With nobody to give me a sign
Just going back - all alone.

Back to an unknown past,
I didn't get rich, didn't become a hero,
But time went by so fast
And now it's back down to zero.

Wild

Part I

I stand in the stables – all alone.
Wondering – how long?
Has this been my home?
Once I would've broken out – when I was strong.
No chains, no door,
Would've held me.
I never thought of what the future had in store
Because I was free…

I was born in the great wild,
In a land of grass and never-ending plains.
Where the summers were warm and the winters mild,
The seasons divided by cool, refreshing rains.
The food was abundant,
The water more so,
Migration was redundant,
And I had a chance to grow.

As I continued growing up,
Life was easy and life was good.
Sometimes it was peaceful, sometimes rough
But I lived like I should.
Sometimes, groups of us would disappear
And never return.
Everybody kept quiet, we were scared,
Especially when the forest started to burn.

They hunted us night and day,
Using ropes to catch us on the run.
None of us got away
Not a single one.
They put us into a round enclosure,
No food or water was given.
We were left in the sun's exposure,
While, hit by stinging whips, we were driven.

Many of us fell during those days
Never to get up again.
It was either starvation, thirst or the sun's rays,
And never one did it rain…
They came to look at us,
Pointed and shouted
And generally made a big fuss;
Then I was ousted.

They threw a rope around my neck
And dragged me away.
I tried to break free but I was a weakened wreck,
There was nothing I could do and nothing I could say.
I never saw my family again,
Alone in such a vast and lonely land.
And I always carried a pain
That nobody would ever understand.

They shoved me into a cage on wheels,
With a tall door and tiny windows.
Not many know how it feels
To have a future that only somebody else knows.
In this cage it was airless and hot
And I put my face next to a slight crack.
I saw many other cages with wheels and what not,
But I could not look back.

I travelled for many hours,
Through wild fields of green
And saw shiny, strange-looking towers.
I thought I had already seen
Everything there was to see,
Until I heard a frightful din.
And it had a strange effect on me,
For suddenly, I knew, my escape I had to begin.

It was dark when I arrived,
The terrible noise had receded
And I had thankfully survived.
Doors were opened and let in air that was much needed.
They led me into a building divided into rows,
And in each one, hay was piled into a heap.
They put me into one and pulled the door to a close.
I stood for a few moments and then fell asleep.

Sleep left early for me, like it always did,
When the sky was still dark
And the darkness hid
Me, the birds only beginning to lark.
I stretched myself out,
Pried open my eyes to the brightening light,
Put my head up and looked about
And what a strange sight!

I could hardly believe my eyes!
And my brain took a while
To finally realize,
As I looked upon row after row, file after file.
They were like me,
Locked away in small wooden stalls
But none of them tried to break free-
Just stood and stared at the nearest walls.

I neighed; I bucked and tried to break the door.
I tried to jump over and made a loud clatter.
I kicked until I couldn't kick anymore
And then I heard a soft patter.
They stood looking at me,
Talking in hushed voices
And to break free
I didn't have many choices.

One of them took out a strange-looking device
And pointed it at my chest.
It looked shiny and wicked – not nice
But I still tried to break out, not taking a rest.
Suddenly there was a popping sound
And I felt a sharp prick.
As I slowly fell to the ground
I thought – was this some kind of trick...?

Woke up with a terrible headache,
Not knowing how much time had gone past,
My brain felt as if somebody was going over it
with a rake
But I had to recover fast.
I had not noticed this before,
But there was something in my mouth – metal
bit.
Didn't know what this was for
And I couldn't get rid of it.

They came to take me away.
Opened the door and led by the strange looking
rope
They took me outside: it was a bright sunny day
And my heart refilled with fresh hope,
For they led me onto a vast green plain –
Filled with grass, flowers and trees.
This sight brought back the pain
As I remembered the grass, swaying in the
breeze.

Only one of them led me,
The rest of them, some distance off, were
waiting
And as I could see,
It was me who they were debating.
I guessed this chance was as good as any,
For deep down, I knew
I didn't have many
So I knew exactly what to do.

Suddenly, I came to a stop,
The one who was leading me, not knowing,
Stumbled and had to drop
The leather strap, as he kept on going.
And before he could recover
I was already galloping away.
Galloping towards the trees cover:
I had escaped! I was on my way!

I galloped until the sun set in the sky –
Until I was far from that place.
Galloping – I felt I could fly
As the sweat poured down my face.
Finally, I stopped in a grove of trees,
Where it was quiet and the air was sweet,
Where a cool evening breeze
Lulled me into sleeping on my feet.

I dreamed of field and grass,
Of soft rolling hills, of my kind.
All my memories seemed to pass,
Being relived in my mind.
Alas, these dreams meant little to me
Because home was a long way off.
But I was alive and I was free
And that was something nobody could scoff.

Sleep was finished before it had begun,
I woke up weak and tired.
As it got brighter – the sun;
I knew my reprieve had expired.
Nibbled some grass, covered in morning dew,
Drank some water from a nearby stream.
In which direction should I go? Nobody knew…
So I did what I always do: I followed my dream.

I started out with a quick trot,
Kept going for many hours, many days.
I would've galloped but it turned hot
And I grew tired in many ways.
But I kept myself going,
Always towards what I thought was home.
Trotting, walking – never slowing
Until I was utterly alone…

Now I could see, now I could tell,
What I had gotten myself into.
Things were definitely not well
And I didn't know what to do.
Wandering in circles: I was lost.
No water, no food…no shade!
Trying to find home at all cost,
As my memories became a hallucinatory parade.

Five days had gone past,
Since I had made my flight.
I didn't know how long I could last
For the sun burned and it was freezing at night.
I thought I saw something in the distance,
But my body was in its final mode
Because I tumbled to earth, at that instance…
Right next to barely visible, dirt road…

Part II

I guess this small part
Is the happiest one.
Although I seemed happy, my heart,
Never truly felt the fun.
I still stood – all alone,
Reminiscing my past:
How close was I to home?
When it all unraveled so fast.

After I collapsed near the dirt track
I don't remember how I survived
But when I thought back:
I knew - without them I would've died,
For when I finally opened my eyes,
To greet a new day
I came to realize
That I was lying amid stacks of hay.

The days passed by:
Too quickly for me
And I don't know why
But I felt free.
They were not like the ones I knew,
They were different in many ways:
About them – I learned something new,
For I lived with them for many days.

Three of them, there were,
Thin, sickly two –legged creatures.
Not only did they not have fur
But also pale and fragile features.
One was obviously the leader,
The other its mate.
The third was the smallest, only about a meter
And whether foal or cub, I'll not debate.

How they got me there, I never found out,
But I guess the four-wheeled thing that made a roar,
Whenever it moved about,
Had been used to carry me from death's door.
About that I don't really care,
For they had saved me: I was alive.
They nursed me back to health, they were fair
And somehow I knew I would survive.

In that short time span
I grew quite attached.
And I could've escaped, I might have ran,
For my gate was never latched.
But I didn't run, I didn't escape,
Because they knew and so did I:
That I was in pretty bad shape,
And if I escaped – I would only die.

But I guess happiness had to end:
It just couldn't last.
I had made a friend
And lost it just as fast.
Termination didn't come from human's hands.
It was something unchangeable, it was too late,
It affected everything – me, my friends, and all the lands.
It was inevitable…it was fate.

It happened on a dark and rainy day.
When everybody was inside.
I didn't know everything would be ripped away
By forces from which nobody could hide.
And as the wind started to gust,
The rain turning into a light mist,
I didn't know that everything I had learnt to trust
Would very soon cease to exist…

Everything happened in a flash,
Before I even had time to realize.
There was a cracking sound and a loud crash:
Then the barn disintegrated before my eyes.
I ran through this maelstrom of debris
Dodging flying pieces of wood.
Then wind howled and I couldn't see
But I did what I could.

As the howling wind subsided
I came to the place
Where my friends had once resided –
Rubble was the only trace…
And I ran as fast as my legs would carry me,
Not wanting to believe it was all gone.
I didn't hear, I didn't see:
Just kept running – on and on…

Part III

I kept running until I fell,
Then everything went pitch black.
When I woke up – it was heaven or hell
But of light there was no lack.
Again I was in a building, in a jail,
With no fresh air to breath.
In my weakened state – escape had to fail,
So I was locked away: never could I leave…

But my prediction was wrong
Because they came to take me away
Before very long,
And led me to a stable filled with hay.
There they left me for a couple of days:
All alone in that pre-fabricated barn
Everyday being given the same oat-filled trays:
This is where I began my yarn…

And you can bet
That I'm not done,
That I'm not finished yet,
Not yet, not this one…
So you better start reading again.
Listen to the wind wail,
Listen to the rain on the window pane,
Listen: as I continue my tale.

After many days of confinement
They had come for me.
I guess they thought I was ready for refinement,
Knowing that I couldn't break free.
They walked me out
And put me into that dreadful wheeled box.
I didn't even have time to look about
As they pushed me in and closed all those locks.

As you might have noticed before
I can run with considerable speed
And what they had in store
Was definitely not what I needed…
I was thrown from side to side in that cage
Until my legs turned to butter.
When this torture finally stopped – I was in a
rage
And my brain seemed to flutter.

They attached me
To a two-wheeled device.
Any more confined I could not be,
And trust me: it wasn't nice.
Then one of them climbed onto that contraption
And took out a metal-tipped whip –
Perhaps for my own "adaption"?
As I felt my hide sting and begin to rip…

I took off at a dead run,
Accented by the whips' crack,
And I didn't stop for anyone:
Kept running round and round that track.
Kept running until I could run no more,
Trying to escape the stinging pain.
Didn't know why, didn't k now what for
But they just kept hitting me, again and again.

I think they were pleased with outcome,
By the way they acted.
They poked me, looked at me and then some
But I was so tired – I couldn't have reacted.
Then they took off that two-wheeled piece of wood
And set it on the ground.
The weight off my shoulders felt good,
Even though I didn't make a sound.

I still remember that day:
The start of my "professional career".
As they would say,
But my soul was always filled with fear.
The next time I was harnessed to that thing
Was in front of a huge crowd
And they were clapping, shouting and starting to sing,
It was all so humiliating, so loud…

That race was just one of many
They put me through.
And I won them all, didn't lose any…
What else could I do?
I guess I was treated ok;
Twice a day I was fed,
Somebody came to brush me every day
And I had lots of hay as my bed.

A day, a month, a year,
Time passed this way.
And now I'm here:
My mane ragged and grey.
I had just won another race,
Another trophy on the wall
In its rightful place,
Next to them all.

But this victory had a cost,
Something all-important, something great.
I wonder if it had been better if I lost
But now it was already too late.
My leg was broken
And even I could tell
That by the way they had spoken
Things were not well.

I lay there, in pain,
With a strange feeling of conclusion.
Outside, it had started to rain.
My life was coming to a close, that was no illusion.
They took out something long and thin;
The rain had started to pour
And I thought of my lost home, my lost kin,
Finally realizing what that needle was for…

My mind drifted through my past,
Flashing images before my eyes
At first slowly, then quite fast.
While outside – rain fell from the skies.
Remembered that human family in the middle of nowhere,
Remembered my family, my friends,
The ones who actually had time to care,
Knowing all the while, this is where it ends…

Then everything started to grow dull and dark,
And my memories began to fade.
But one thought kept on glowing – like a spark,
And it wasn't the "life" I had "made",
It was when I was wild and free,
When I had life pulsing through me
But now I just lay there…lifeless and cold.
Finally…my story has been told…

Firework

Firework

Launched and flying
Faster and faster
Not even trying
Being its own master.

Higher and higher
Into the sky
No chain, no wire
No reason not to fly.

It seems it'll never stop
Keep going forever
Never going to fall, never drop
No failures; never…

Almost through the atmosphere
And into space
Who cares where?
Just leave this place

But its destiny is pre-decided
Nothing it can do
Somebody already presided
Everything for you.

And so it explodes in a ball of flame
Its life snuffed out.
But where to put the blame?
Wait! What are we talking about?
Some little rocket in the sky
Whose only purpose was to brilliantly, die…

Other Side

Nobody knows
How close
It really is

Just over the cleft
Not right, not left
Just this

It's just a few yards
But will you play your cards
And leap over this crack?

Everything you ever wished for,
Everything…and more:
Everything that you ever need.

It's waiting for you.
All you have to do
Is jump

Like a shining light,
A much better sight
Than this dump

Are you afraid to try?
Scared that you might die
And hold yourself back?

But who can resist the
temptation?
And miss the sensation
Of no lack?

All of it – it can't hide
Waiting for you on the other
side
But will you take heed…?

Man in the Mirror

The man in the mirror is looking at me
And I don't believe what my eyes see,
Nothing left of what I was,
And all of this because…?

Dry, drooping skin
I look so sickly and thin
Wrinkles around my eyes
This has to be some sort of disguise!

Time couldn't go by so fast
I've had no life, no past
And everywhere I look, everywhere I go
There's absolutely nobody I know

Not a single solitary friend
In a world so big and grand
And it's already close to the end
Nobody here - I don't understand

All the diamonds and all the gold,
All the money I ever made,
Couldn't buy me anything and now I'm old.
Just a man in a mirror and even that starts to fade.

Perfect

Perfect…who ever was?
Nobody is really the same,
We all have our flaws
And it doesn't matter from where we came.

We all look for the mistakes,
For something bad.
But do we have what it takes?
To look at what we had.
To look a different way,
No matter what they say.

We try to look for every flaw,
For something untrue.
But can we forget that "unwritten law"?
And look through…
If not, then you'll never find a friend
Even if you keep searching till the end.

Perfect…are you?
Are you "Hercules", a computer whiz?
Admit that even you're not perfect – it's true.
And if nobody's perfect…who really is?

Automatic

I get up every morning
At six-forty-five.
Stretching and a yawning
As I struggle to strive
Getting out of my bed
And clearing the cobwebs out of my head.

Splash water on my face,
Brush my teeth,
And the toothpaste's minty taste
Feels like a relief.
Brushing until my gums hurt,
Pulling on my pants and shirt.

Have a bit to eat,
Pile the dishes in the sink,
And already I'm on the street
Without even having to think
About opening the door…
Hey! Who needs that for?

Get on the city metro,
Read the newspaper on the way:
Murder, drugs and fashion going retro –
The things I read every single day.
The subway starts slowing down – where?
I already know: I'm already there…

I ride the elevator to my office block,
Up to the 21st floor.
It's already eight o' clock
As I open the door.
Desks stand row upon row
And I walk – greeting people I don't even know…

Sit down on my plastic chair
And boot up my PC.
I'd say there's not enough air
But who'll care about me?
A hundred people in a single room
Really feels like impending doom…

Tapping away at my keyboard
Tap, click, tap, and tap:
It's already automatic and I feel bored,
While my spine is getting closer to my lap.
Staring at my computer screen,
I'm starting to see only green…

Time for my lunch break…
Wait! What? It's already two o' clock?
Drink coffee with my "friends" – to stay awake.
Talk about politics, terrorism and stock.
Ask automatic questions
And give robotic directions…

Back to my computer, back to work,
Still boring as ever
But at least the coffee dispersed the murk
And made me notice the weather…
Waiting for the work-day to be done
And I'm not the only one…

This day's finished, it's 6pm.
I crowd into the subway
With the rest of them…
Almost crushed amid the fray.
But finally I'm alone
As I approach my "home".

Climb up to my 3rd floor apartment
And open its shabby door.
Grab some food from the fridge compartment
And stack my clothes on the floor.
Turn on my color TV
And watch a random channel that's free…

Watching until my eyes start to droop
And I feel even worse than before.
The picture seems to loop
But I don't care anymore.
My skull feels like it's full of lead
As I drag myself towards my bed…

Automatically kick off my shoes
And fall back.
Don't remember today, don't remember the news:
My mind is just black.
And as soon my head hits the pillow, I sleep,
Sleep until tomorrow's wake-up beep…

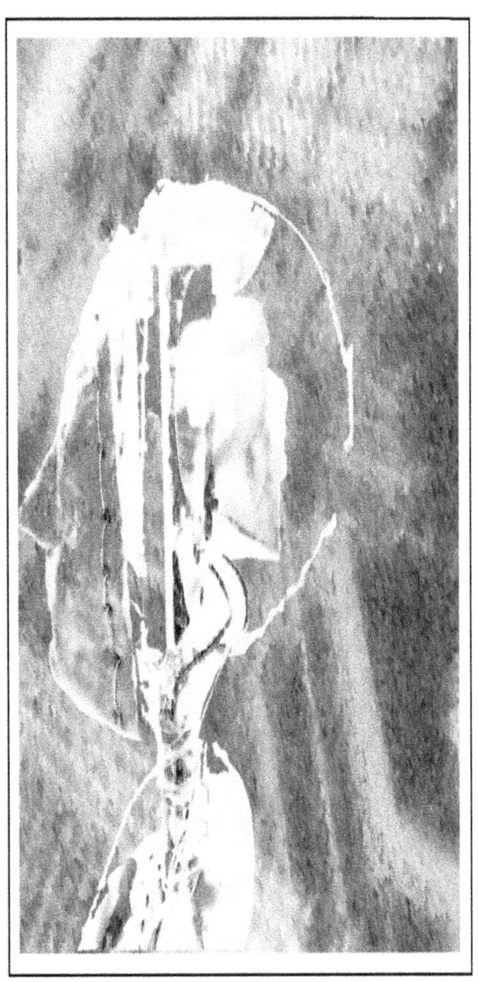

The Fear

Did you ever feel the fear?
Sensed something over there,
Lurking in the shadows,
Something nobody knows

Have you ever felt? - that whatever you do,
There is always something watching you
Always something watching you from the dark
When you're walking down the street, in the park

And when you're walking all alone - without a sound
You feel something and you turn around
And there's nowhere to hide, nowhere to flee
But there's nothing there, nothing to see

But you can't stop your sixth sense
Can't stop from feeling so tense
Can't stop from seeing those evil eyes leer
Can't stop from being infected by the fear.

Tomorrow Can Wait

We live, we work,
We try to see through the murk
And we always hurry
To think about what's going to be
And always quick to worry
About something we don't yet see.

Living with a sense of dread
Floating above our head
Worrying about something not yet done
Anxious about something being concealed,
Concealed in the track we run,
Waiting until everything is revealed.

Living in constant fear
Scared of something over "there",
But we don't have to live like this,
Don't have to hesitate.
Think of all the things we'd miss
If we don't let tomorrow wait.

Sand

Grains of sand,
On lives' beach
Life? Who's to understand?
When it's so out of reach.

The wind blows them away,
The waves wash them out.
Who is going to say,
What this is about...?

Piling up in calm weather,
Being swept away by a hurricane.
Who knows what is better,
Burning sun or freezing rain?

Older sand is buried by the new,
This process repeated again and again.
Purpose? Who knows and who ever knew?
'cause nobody knows what happens then...

A never-ending cycle of replacement, of substitution;
Taking hundreds of years
For just one stage of evolution
But it's just sand, who really cares?

Grains of sand, unnoticeable under your feet.
So tiny, who would call them grand?
Facing cold water and desert heat
But are we really talking about sand...?

Chasing Rainbows

I walk on these grass plains
The earth soaked by the spring rains
I watch the cloud go along its path
Inflicting its drenching wrath

Suddenly in the sky, a rainbow
I envision a pot of gold
It will be there at last - I know
Or at least that's what I've been told

I stumble towards all those colors - arched
My legs are weak, my throat parched
I can almost see the rainbows' end
Just over that hill, around that bend

But then the rainbow disappears
Right before my eyes - now filled with tears
But again I start to run
Because I think I saw another one.

Free-Falling

Falling through the sky,
The ground seems so far below
And I feel like I can fly.
But little do I know,
That I'm falling so fast,
That this free-fall won't last.

But right now I'm way up high,
The wind rushing past me.
But I don't know that my eyes lie,
That they don't see what they have to see,
That, into the ground - I will smash,
That, soon - I will crash.

And when I finally become aware,
When I finally understand,
That I can't get away from here,
That I have nowhere to land.
That I cannot stall
My speeding free-fall.

I realize I don't have wings,
And my parachute doesn't eject.
I don't have any of these things,
And there's nothing to do, nothing to collect.
The ground rushes up before my eyes,
And I look up one last time: at the clear blue
skies.

The Flood

Water rushes by me,
Trying to rip me away,
As I hold on to the trunk of a tree:
Rushing, pulling, all day.

I keep holding on,
Not letting go.
I won't last long,
At least that, I know;
But my hands are frozen in their grip,
Not realizing that they can slip.

Life is truly strange,
Nothing can be expected,
A sudden change
And you're the one being dissected.
Just when you thought you had something going,
It's wiped out, without you even knowing…

Just a few hours ago,
Everything was fine.
How could I know?
That life would "cross the line",
That a wall of water would come
And I would be paralyzed, numb…

My life, my dog, my home…
My family, my job, my car:
Gone…and now I'm alone
When hope is so far.
All that I lived for…
Swept out the door.

I see things floating by
But I don't care.
I look for hope or at least I try,
But it's not there.
My brain is set on 'replay',
Set on this terrible day.

Night starts to fall:
The flood is only stronger.
I keep thinking of it all,
Knowing I can't hold on much longer.
I see my fingers letting go
And I can't stop them, can't stop the flow.

One by one they lose their grip
And finally I slowly slip,
Thinking of what I lost,
Everything; achieved at such a cost,
Gone, in a single day:
The flood…just swept it all away.

Simple Man

Don't need the house in the hills,
Don't need the garage-full of luxury cars,
Don't need the expensive diet pills,
I just need a sky full of stars.

Don't need a private plane
Or my own servant.
I'll still be the same,
Only more observant.

Don't want the fancy four-post bed,
Don't need a bathroom that's a thousand square feet.
Just need somewhere to lay my head
And make ends meet.

Don't need all the gold, all the riches,
Only a few dollars I can save,
And my clothes are full of stitches.
(I still can't take everything to my grave…)

Just enough for today and maybe tomorrow
But at least I have something and it's mine.
Never had to borrow
And I am still fine…

Everything simple as can be:
No instructions, no layout, no plan…
Living life as it comes to me,
Living life: like a simple man…

Nothing's going to come to you
So don't stand around too long
You may think it's right, or it's wrong
But nothing's going to fall out of the blue

Do what you have to do
Go where you have to go
Live life like it suits you
Know what you want to know

Go Get It

Get up and get moving
Get up and do some proving
Prove that you are right
And be the one who steps into the spotlight

They say nothing in life is free
But that doesn't really mean
That you can't get up and be seen
And be who you want to be.

Watch the Sunrise

The night is over,
The darkness gone,
And hope is so much closer
To being turned on.

There's more light,
With every passing second
Soon, day will be built from night,
Much sooner than we reckoned.

The first rays of the sun,
We can already see.
Finishing everything ever begun,
Back to what it should be.

Almost over the top,
It's almost a new day
And we don't want it to stop
Chasing the darkness away.

We laugh, we cry,
Our feelings - we don't disguise
As the darkness leaves the sky
And makes way for a glorious sunrise.

www.ingramcontent.com/pod-product-compliance
Ingram Content Group UK Ltd.
Pitfield, Milton Keynes, MK11 3LW, UK
UKHW020236250726
13967UKWH00001B/398